Praise for *The Things Downriver*

All the fire that drives us, or consumes us, happens by about age 8, and the act of mapping the textures of the ephemeral landscape of childhood is an act of personal myth building, of liberation; an alchemical act. Reading *The Things Downriver* is to watch an artist individuate before our very eyes taking us along for the ride with the taste of homemade ravioli and two fingers of grappa poured from the goatskin bag.

In this era when some would demonize immigrants, here is not only an archeologist of morning digging into her own family's immigration but as a grown woman, now the age of grandmothers, discovering via mapping how becoming a daughter works in USAmerica. *The Things Downriver* is an act of alchemy with the power to transform its readers. All literature should aim for this, but Denise Calvetti Michaels has accomplished it.

—Paul E. Nelson
Author of *A Time Before Slaughter, American Sentences, American Prophets*

Does memory have a rhythm when we are remembering? For Denise Calvetti Michaels, remembering is never having remembered, but rather mapping, finding "the things downriver." Language rises up to make meaning and is sometimes buttonholed casting its surprising skins: "*fig*, how it becomes incident, episode and commotion…indigo skins broken in the dusty dirt." A meditation on summers spent with her family on her grandparents' farm—emigrants from the Piedmont area in northern Italy—Michaels repeatedly discovers how sensory experience leads to the formation of an ephemeral, oscillating identity: "We are the memory of those summers." "I didn't know that someday I would understand that the afternoon light, its angle against the window-pane, was essential to the way we saw ourselves." While this meditation never lets go of the desire for abundance, it also contemplates paucity and memory's potential falseness. "Perhaps this is a statement of abundance compared to my grandparents' former poverty of place, Montaldo Scarampi, the village where in the summer small boys stand naked to the wall and pee the dust to life." "Maybe I exaggerate the habitat of my childhood, the sustenance of those early years, using language as a decoy to protect it, the sentence a lure." The brilliant beauty of *The Things Downriver* is its melodic phrasing, one word leading to another, an unfolding that bends the staunch subject and predicate expectations of standard English in pursuit of its own lyricism.

—Jeanne Heuving, author of *Mood Indigo*

洞月亮

CAVE MOON PRESS
YAKIMA 中 WASHINGTON

2020

© Copyright 2020 Denise Calvetti Michaels
All rights reserved.
Cover Art: Denise Calvetti Michaels
Book Design: Doug Johnson

ISBN: 978-0-9797785-7-5

Acknowledgments

Grateful acknowledgment is made to the following publications, in which poems in this book were previously published.

King County Poetry on Buses: ***Your Body of Water,*** curated by Jourdan Imani Keith, ("There are Things Downriver I've Never Properly Grieved," 2017.)

Yours Truly, ("Once My Grandmother Walks Us," "Farm is the Language of Gesture," "Two Interludes Bookend the Experience," and "When I Begin the Light is a Sheaf," 2017-2018.)

Clamor, (Where is the Map?" "The Lyric is the Desire to Breathe," "We Were Sent Outside," and "The Water Given," 2018-2019.)

Crosscurrents, ("In the Beginning, Glint of Sunrise Low on the Horizon," 2019.)

Mapping the Dream: A Poetics of Remembering

The prose notebook is something else entirely, without repetition or revision included. It is anti-memoir, a response to a day, and all the day produces by chance. It is in many ways the most radical form: a chronicle without a rhythm or a beat. Pure reflection, transparency. No audience desired or expected. It is inherently anarchist.

— Fanny Howe *The Winter Sun: Notes on a Vocation*

I wrote a lyric of remembering when I was a girl visiting my grandparents' farm in Salinas, California, with my younger brother Dennis for the summer.

To finish the book has been a long haul, because of the many steps or stages, each embedded with emotional content dredged to the surface by remembering, both bittersweet as well as revelatory, and inaccessible except through the act of writing.

A long haul because this was a book I wanted to write for many years but struggled with form. Finding the form gave me permission to construct acts of remembering that came to me in sequences / vignettes as I didn't know what I would be remembering until I began to write.

I also worried whether I could sustain the work, uncertain there was enough substance to my remembering to shape into creative writing. Becoming "process oriented" kept me from abandoning the farm as the territory of my work.

And there may have been multiple creative processes going on – 1) daily writing; 2) shaping the daily work into a book; 3) standing up for the work's potential to have meaning; and 4) the development of myself as a writer who conceptualizes why and how to tap an aesthetic space through acts of writing and remembering.

My paternal grandparents, Agostina and Ercole Bianco, immigrated to the United States, May 24, 1910, as a young married couple from Montaldo Scarampi, a small village near Asti in the Piedmont vineyard country of northern Italy. They were part of the wave of Southern and Eastern European emigrants to the United States between 1892 and the mid-1920's—immigrants who became miners, farmers, and workers in factories and construction. My grandparents worked long days, aspiring to care for their farm well into their nineties.

I wrote *The Things Downriver* to map the dream, to pay homage to summers on the farm in Salinas, and to validate through writing what I was conjuring: recollections of childhood sensory experiences embedded within the memories of infancy, childhood and early adolescence during visits to the farm for holidays, family gatherings, and summertime when my brother and I were left to the supervision of our grandparents. Old photos show me as a wide-eyed baby girl dressed in bonnets, pinafores and hand-knit sweaters in the arms of my elders.

The idea for the way remembering begins within sensorial landscapes was developed by French poet, Yves Bonnefoy, in his essay, *The Place of Grasses:*

Poetry is the memory of those instants of presence, of plenitude experienced during the years of childhood, followed by the apprehension of non-being underlying those instants which becomes translated as doubt, and then by that hesitation that constitutes life; but it is also a reaffirmation, it is our willing that there should be meaning at the moment meaning falls away.

Bonnefoy's writing focus rooted in childhood also parallels William Wordsworth's poem, *Intimations of Immortality*.

The process of writing triggered remembering and the act of writing, even when I didn't know where it might lead, allowed me to reach the places I was mapping within the dreamscape. The more I pursued remembering, the more I became obsessed by the generative act of writing that unfurled the act of remembering, an organic reciprocity. I soon realized this was *mapping*, different and deeper than mere "dreaming." Mapping involved allowing myself time to reimagine a series of experiences, as I collected memories of detailed episodes that haunted me and lead to further memories. In a way, I was re-experiencing the past, and in so doing creating the more elaborate constructions of neural pathways for remembering.

Toi Derricotte expressed it simply and more elegantly, perhaps, when she wrote, "Memory is in the service of the greatest psychic need."

Works Cited

http://immigrationtounitedstates.org/588_immigration_act_of_1917.html.

Yves Bonnefoy, *The Arriere-pays*, The Place of Grasses, p. 191, Translated by Stephen Romar, Seagull Press, Calcutta, India, 2012.

Yves Bonney, *Second Simplicity, New Poetry & Prose, 1991-2011*; translated by Hoyt Rogers, Yale University Press, 2012.

Fanny Howe, *The Winter Sun: Notes on a Vocation*, Graywolf Press, Saint Paul, Minnesota, 2009.

The Things Downriver

Denise Calvetti Michaels

But does it matter to which category her piece belongs, falling as it did inside her journal?

How much came from the daily bread of dream, imagination, reading, and life itself all combined?
—Fanny Howe, *Wedding Dress*

Home is that youthful region where a child is the only real living inhabitant. Parents, siblings, and neighbors, are mysterious.apparitions, who come, go, and do strange unfathomable things in and around the child, the regions' only enfranchised citizen.
—Maya Angelou, *Letter to my Daughter*

The prose notebook is something else entirely, without repetition or. revision included. It is anti-memoir, a response to a day, and all the day produces by chance. It is in many ways the most radical form: a chronicle without a rhythm or a beat. Pure reflection, transparency. No audience desired or expected. It is inherently anarchist.
—Fanny Howe, *Winter Sun*

The human unit of time is the space between a grandfather's memory of his own childhood and a grandson's knowledge of those memories as he heard about them.
—Ralph Blum, from *Blackberry Winter*, Margaret Mead

Part One

I remember the syncopation of leaves, bruised apples,
language burning bittersweet charms on my tongue, the farm in the
distance, mapping the dream.

We were children absorbing the world.

We were children crawling under trees, observing ant hills and the wasp nest high in the willow, the mound of dirt with its mammal that peered out at dusk.

We crisscrossed existence on four-acres, invisible histories that will dwell later in the dream of the farm.

Ancestors we did not realize were the bamboo's rustlings roamed among us.

Confounded by the sun's disappearance the field of vision transformed the sky salmon pink bleeding orange colors.

In the beginning, glint of sunrise low on the horizon.

Cirrus clouds infuse the palette of arid places, sienna-bronze-copper-dun.

I know this because my father stopped the car on the shoulder of the road.

Teaching us to observe how dawn broke in stages, a sequence of moments, some blinding, others subtle and the terrain gradually emerged with shape and sound.

We were all together, new oil change, tank full of gasoline, the Coleman stove and a good map, heading on the highway to daybreak.

We were driving toward morning, over the ridge worn thin within the folds of road maps to Yosemite, Arroyo Seco and Paso Robles.

I must have been carried to the car and fallen back asleep, waking later to find myself in the backseat, my brother beside me, asking, what did I dream?

Once he slid across the seat when the car veered too sharply and we landed together giggling on the floor. Duck feathers from a pillow fight the night before sticking to our tongues and sweaty faces. Then we'd force ourselves to regain composure and gaze out the window watching our reflections side by side in the glass, two siblings born a year apart in November,
Dennis the Scorpio, Denise a Sagittarius.

We didn't know it then but we were paying attention, eyes peeled, as we listened to our father speak English to his friend Ray from childhood, then switch to the Piedmontese dialect of his ancestors to address my grandfather, Ercole Angelo Bianco, who arranged to take the day off knowing someone would water and feed the animals.

Road trips began early because our father was accustomed to work on the dairy.

To map this place is to conjure cougar, bobcat and coyote, my father a boy who raised an abandoned fawn, then let her go.

I am the memory of those summers.

On my desk near my computer screen a photo of my brother. On the back: *This is me! On top of Half Dome! Three thousand feet straight down!*

The family myth, I always protect him, give him what he wants.

I would describe the dream this way: sensation of swerving to avoid owls breaching the moon.

When I was born my parents rented a house on Bernal Drive, a doll house compared to the farm on Natividad that turned onto Bernal a handful of miles on the outskirts.

I was born in Salinas. It's important to say I lied about my place of birth before I understood why. I hope this composition pays homage, to redeem the place, though I don't fault the girl.

There are things people listen to you say and don't want to hear because their own memories are triggered.

Grandfather's friend for example, Pisano from the Old Country, both men from the same region in Northern Italy, who tells me at the fishing camp, no, thank you, he wouldn't like a piece of my grandmother's chicken because he's eaten so much chicken it no longer tastes good to him.

Something I can't imagine, living so long that the taste for a favorite food is gone; but what is spoken with his eyes is that his wife is dead, he lives alone and the past is a dry river of stones.

My father transfixed by Yosemite.

He returned with us to camp along the Merced River and to hike the Tuolumne Meadows, compelled to take relatives who visit from Italy, WWII buddies from the Navy who drove out with wives and children to California.

It's difficult to separate myself from his story, to know if wilderness belongs to me because of him and those family road trips.

I remember the nightly fire-fall embers pushed off Glacier Point, though the tradition was discontinued long ago.

I remember the legend of lost boy Elmer whose name, called out by campers, echoed at dusk from the valley floor.

What I map is the *textures* of an ephemeral landscape, planks beside the river burning, acorn and twig, feather molting.

I write in minor key, over there, running, outside the back door, down three steps, toward the weeping willow.

Wandering culverts, we dragged our toes through gravel, hiding out, far away from the house with the Spanish tile roof and adobe walls.

We never used the front door.

And if the doorbell rings, it's a stranger, sometimes a kind Jehovah's Witness who doesn't know us, and never will.

Ancestors we did not realize were the bamboo's rustlings roamed among us.

I write about what craves the lyric.

Silver strands brushed back with her hands tattered with chicken feathers she's plucking in a vat of hot water also used to wash clothes.

And, the gunny sack on the floor to dry bleating newborn lambs by the stove.

Gashed thigh she sutured herself ashamed of going to the emergency room and later my father's anger because she did not go to the hospital.

Heartbreak, when she came to spray the bedroom for mosquitoes and turn down the covers because I don't remember my grandmother smiling, wearing lipstick or rouge, earrings or hairpins though there is the photo glued to her Certificate of Naturalization when she became a U.S. citizen that proves otherwise.

And the valise Agostina used spring of 1911 to carry her belongings aboard the ship named the *Berlin,* Genoa to Ellis Island, is real as the gladiola she cultivated in the garden near the window.

There are no journals or diaries handwritten by women like my grandmother living on the edge of town.

I remember the syncopation of leaves, bruised apples, language burning bittersweet charms on my tongue, the farm in the distance, mapping the dream.

Some things my mother told me, that I was born by caesarian with an owl outside the window while she was in labor.

I write about things that long for what we do not have, hold us together on the map, the girl, the territory of her family, evidence of their tracks.

Summer when I was a girl living on the farm located on Natividad Road my grandparents owned for the last four decades of their lives in the outskirts of Salinas.

The sensory impels my story because when I awoke from this reverie I had been digging with bare hands for traces of our existence in the fertile black dirt that Salinas Valley is famous for.

Maybe I exaggerate the habitat of my childhood, the sustenance of those early years, using language as a decoy to protect it, the sentence a lure. I do remember a rural landscape that lives and breathes.

Memories enlarge interiors, bottle nicked open, grappa dregs in goatskin, riffs that never resolve.

Synapses fire. Neurons communicate across the gap.

The bridge each neural message must cross to carry bits and pieces, but since dendrites do not actually touch, to transmit memory involves taking a leap. Trillions of synaptic gaps convey what is fluid and malleable; memory turning into consciousness as dreams and fragments.

Emotions arise I don't want to call depression rather the bittersweet melancholy associated with the matrix of memory to remind the place has meaning.

Walking the park today I remember vivid colors and sepia tones, recollections channeled through the Brownie black and white's my mother affixed to pages inside the album monogramed with my initials, same as my brother.

Sometimes each photo is a fresh start; Redwood City house when I'm two, El Camino above the grocery store when my family first left Salinas, yet so few of me on the farm. Especially during the summer when our mother helps with the store, mourns the death of her father, travels with her mother to reconnect with the side of the family that never left Italy.

When emotional terrain takes over I veer off road to a set of givens: fence post and barbwire, bamboo thicket and irrigation ditch—hiding places, I realize now, where I marked the map of my childhood so that this four-acre farm is held in consciousness long enough to pin down.

But here, on the two-dimensional plane of white paper, I'm doomed, my sentence failing the dream I imagine as densely rich etymological layering within a sequence of interludes of which I know only my share, given a particular bent to excavate this landscape.

So, if I did have a box of photos, perhaps the elderly neighbors I observed remove sunshine-scented cotton sheets off the line.

And the barefoot Filipina girl who held a bundle of rhubarb wrapped in newsprint and walked over from across the road with her mother in the afternoons to trade for eggs.

Circle of wooden crates for the men spitting tobacco, told to go inside, not to look, rooster forced head-first into a gunny sack.

Scent of fish oil, chili peppers, rice, left to the weather in the cemetery.

The day Dennis takes aim with the rifle, not realizing it's loaded.

Alone at the park, when older boys try to push me off the slide and I would have broken an arm rather than let them succeed.

Poker, accordion songs, bocce ball; up late, listening.

There are things people listen to you say and walk away.

It triggers memory, and this is painful; tools and routines of a farm are a way to anchor.

I wrote this piece because I wanted to write about the things downriver.

Part Two

Farm is the language of gesture within the space of my mother's absence, a benign neglect because of the sensory richness.

Black earth matted to the soles of our shoes and bare feet.

Mud that clings to the roots when we pull up carrots, dig for potatoes, beets we rinse in the sink stopped with brown water.

Backdoor stoop, basking with honeysuckle we will fight over trying to make perfume for our mother who is in Italy.

Action word *farming* that lured me and my brother outside.

Chain link bamboo property line my brother and I peer through to find bowls of cooked rice left behind by relatives of the deceased on smooth river stones in the Chinese cemetery next door, the only familiar landmark for me that remains, the land for the cemetery purchased with a $100 gold piece around 1901.

The word *fig,* how it becomes incident, episode and commotion leading to story of wasps circling pulpy seed, indigo skins broken in the dusty dirt.

Mid-afternoons, Grandmother in the herb garden, hemmed in with boxwood, gathering flowers to change the vase she arranges with carnation, dahlia and zinnia for the statue of the Madonna in the alcove, rosary beads dangling from her hands.

Grandfather's patience tested, late August, walking toward us, Toscano cigar stub between his teeth, brown paper bag to gesture we pick up the ripe figs off the ground, my brother's squishing with his bare feet.

My grandmother walks us, hand-in-hand, to the dusty rodeo grounds one mile from the farm on Natividad. We played here many summers, staying with our paternal grandparents who lived near Salinas Memorial Hospital where I was born and where she did not go when she fell on the porch steps and cut her leg against the boot scraper. We are too young to understand why she hesitates before entering the grocery store, doubting her broken English, the clerk who rings up the order, bags her groceries, ice cream, peanut butter we should have done without; she and my grandfather known for organic gardening before it has a name. This is about what we discover wandering the property; fig trees, apple orchard, strawberries and wild blackberries, garlic, celery, onions, tomatoes, escarole, romaine, kale, collard greens and string beans we plant and water ourselves; the double-yoke brown eggs we collect, the rabbits in hutches, the rosemary and thyme, basil and carnations, the home grown larder I conjure to remember colors and shapes juxtaposed within the garden, borders and rows and rows of scents and tastes, vertical lattices, their braided honeysuckle patterns tantalizing. Perhaps this is a statement of abundance compared to the my grandparents' former poverty of place, Montaldo Scarampi, the village where in the summer small boys stand naked to the wall and pee the dust to life.

We were sent outside to get along so we fought where sun pooled and honeysuckle tangled and we plucked the blossoms one by one and tasted then squeezed the nectar into tiny glass medicine vials we'd been given by the elderly neighbor in a wheelchair who stayed in the house to tend cats. It ended badly. Another fight over who did what to gather the stamens to make perfume for our mother who was in Italy.

A story came out of it from the old country, Agostina's village, *Blame is an ugly animal, no one wants him,* and the word I never heard her use again, *cattivo*, meaning, caught by the devil, someone bad, wicked, naughty, in reference to my brother, little guy I adored and defended.

In the afternoon we slither along the creek bottom using our hands to anchor our bodies to the smooth boulders covered with slick algae. We net crayfish. Dislodge minnows. Cool boulders sooth our sunburned skin, children who sat in the backseat of our grandparent's '51 Chevy upholstered with horsehair that scratched the backs of our thighs, calamine in the first aid kit in the glove box.

Once we leave for home early with no time to enjoy the picnic my grandmother prepared the night before standing at the stove to fry chicken and rainbow trout, marinate finger-length anchovies in olive oil and garlic she minced with the curved blade of the *mezzaluna*.

I only remember the confusion of mason jars and cotton tablecloth hurriedly thrown together in the backseat after my father hit his head on a rock when he dove in the river, forgetting its depth in late August, and suddenly the road is heavy Sunday afternoon traffic.

We are the memory of those summers.

There are things I will never know.

My grandparents were born in a small Italian village before coming here, not enough ground corn *polenta* to go around, so they marry and move to America.

Maybe it isn't necessary to go to school to learn the orbits of planets or the names of constellations; just that the Milky Way is home, a way of ordering.

In the afternoon hues of honey over the landscape milk from the sun's rays blanching the four-acre patch with color schemes I've since known only in memories.

Farm more than farm.

36 **Fig tree planting with Ercole and Agostina Bianco**

Family Photo (Only one)

With Ercole and Agostina Bianco

Dad

Denise on the farm

Yosemite

Yosemite camping

There are things downriver I've never properly grieved.

That boulder, for example, on the bottom of the river I want to take a jackhammer to fracture into fragments that will glitter the horizon, cat with green eyes on the outcropping staring at me, and I'll tell you I saw it first, the right to dream it, a way of writing.

By dawn, so much is forgiven.

I make mistakes of not concentrating yet I learn what I need to do as I remember and it is clear I mean many things to you so don't force me not to love you; this is how becoming a daughter works.

Two interludes bookend the experience of my father in my life, and hold things together, appear linear, but are not and will never be.

Mapping memory, one sentence at a time that leads back to dredge. For now, a map of a road trip with a beginning and an end. I'm standing before you, impatient to run off to school. Maybe you have a flashback to barefoot girls in pinafores thin as whispers in the one-room school house of your childhood, and you ask yourself how you became the father to this girl wearing shoes and new dresses? On the other side of the river the wind rustles the cottonwood leaves.

Housing developments eventually gouge the landscape; each parcel renamed for the wildness I experienced first-hand living the velocity of a girl who doesn't know at the time what she'll remember is not for sale; no one can divvy.

Ancestors we did not realize were the bamboo's rustlings roamed among us.

Haunted by the face of each ancestor, I lose hours dwelling on a single gesture, trying to make eye contact with an elder crossing the ocean. I shuffle through old photos and commemorative prayer cards of the deceased. I listen to my mother's written and oral histories she takes the time to share, though unlike me, she didn't stay on a farm in Salinas with her grandparents, June through September, many summers of her childhood. I try to make meaning from original documents, late at night, when I'm alone, working at the table with the box I've opened that contains the remnants of the most fragile, the crazed, the delicately faded, trying to offer a liniment, the salve of understanding to quell the losses, soothing and saving the memories.

Again, I'm in the clutch of remembering.

And what triggers is merely the crunch of tires, braking to stop, on gray-flecked gravel.

Scrappy sound of a spin out on the private road entrance to the farm as my father steers the car a bit too sharply off Natividad and slowly past the first of two neighbors' houses, then sudden lurch to the left onto the driveway.

This is how the skid of loose rock becomes the origin sound as synapses fire in the queue, unfurl tendril vines that will detour, surprise and shock, tentacle in directions I may not foresee.

Here, I had a choice of direction in order to locate my grandmother.

Yes, here, when I'm age eight, I would already know she made countless daily forays from the back porch door, as she momentarily left behind the smoky wood stove kitchen to walk out to the dark cool cave of the cold storage room across the way from the house lit by a single overhead bulb.

Within the sanctuary of the cave's four adobe walls my grandmother stored mason jars on long open wood shelves anchored above the freezer's larder of butcher-wrapped beef and lamb, duck and chicken, rabbit, pork and the venison of elk and deer.

I knew of her skill at provisioning because in one compartment of the freezer it became my job to help to store the ravioli she taught me to roll out with the three-foot long rolling pin I keep to explain our legacy to the most recent grandchild who reaches the milestone to understand how food is made within the fold of generations.

Though she's been gone over three decades there is her signature gesture like the marble-sculptured pose of a complex woman.

I see her in this dream in the context of Carrara marble, the *Pieta*.

She wipes her forehead with her apron, carries a basket, a tray, a box, a sack, back and forth, between here and there, two locations she inhabited that belonged to her.

Whatever she carries, she balances; glass jars against the fleeting nature of childhood, juggling the physicality of abundance with the generativity of the magical landscape.

When I imagine her, it is an attempt to understand this aesthetic, palpable, real, beyond words, the hand in motion. Maybe I should simply describe her hands, sketched before I write, in the way Michelangelo sketched drawings before sculpting.

I remember the feel of the cold metal handle of the ravioli wheel she placed in my grasp; how the silver wheel spun, spinning through dough. My brother impatient to play, misapply its function: mince an earthworm, chop tomato limbs. *Spetta* / wait! *Uno momento* / one moment! *Senti* / hear this!

The wheel sings after we daub ravioli filling on the sheets of rolled dough with the mixture of chopped parsley, ricotta and parmesan cheese, ground chicken and fresh-from-the-garden sage, thyme, rosemary.

Theatrics of space transformed; the kitchen, dining room and spare bedroom used to dry the ravioli on table tops and beds draped with clean cotton towels and dusted with flour to prevent sticking.

When we woke in the morning, having slept on the divan, we found dozens of ravioli bagged in bread wrappers tied with double knot to prevent freezer burn. Sometimes, we ate them raw, before falling asleep.

Back and forth, with a rhythm throughout the day, my grandmother on a mission to prepare, preserve, prepare, preserve.

I first heard the word *vaquero* walking down Natividad Road to the rodeo grounds with my grandmother and brother.

We were walking because she never learned to drive the car.

Maybe she whispered to me in dialect, *vaqueros, vaqueros, di la*—over there, or guttural *scat, you!*, my grandmother's ability to accent that thing I should attend to, three muscular horses, sixteen hands, galloping toward us, salt-rimed withers, cinched leather saddles, ruddy men, reddish brown hands holding whips, chestnut manes, burnished flanks, three abreast, Nona speaking to me, not my brother, the word *vaquero* a triptych with doors for three distinct riders outrunning shadows cast by the eucalyptus arcing Natividad, stage for remembrance, the past careening into the future where there is no safe hiding place, riders unyielding, horses surging forward like time and the story of what to tell the granddaughter so she can transcribe the dictation of an immigrant woman, of what to tell granddaughter so she will know the heart of the woman who saved for a piece of land in America.

I'm lost again, wrapped up in my sentences, and forgot to save.

Now I can't return to where I was in the reverie asking myself what she meant as she held my hand and walked me, walking with me and my younger brother, down the road to the rodeo grounds because she didn't know how to drive and because another wouldn't or couldn't take us that afternoon, and so she grabbed her *borsetta*, the purse with the black handle over her arm, and away we walked out of the protection of the niche drive and onto the wild of Natividad, the thoroughfare I would grow to obsess over, thinking for years that my grandparents had only lived here when in fact there had been many way stations in which they were tenants of the ranch, the dairy, the plot, the plat, with a daily schedule to fulfill around the clock, year-long, until the owner decided to develop the land, uprooting them.

Sometimes, I realize the same woman I recall vividly is also the one with whom I never held a long conversation, yet the receiver of her goodness, a girl going along for the ride, the cinema of her life filming around the clock and I'm one of the inhabitants no bigger than a prairie dog or vole, another creature she must have wondered about and fed leaving crumbs beside the back door step.

Who is this woman and how did she shape the one I've become, woman who writes to create a meal, woman who keeps returning to the dining room table with platters of risotto, lasagna, embedded knowledge. Who is the girl she impressed with the language of sensory—connecting emotions to words though there will be a trunk load of experiences the girl will never explore with the woman, and only later will the girl shake out each embroidered item to watch the questions tumble from the folds, photographs, the cinema of memory, the girl and the summer, when they walked to the rodeo and in synch stepped aside for three *vaqueros*.

I recall variegated patterns of seeds, bean seeds shaped like ovals smooth as pebbles on the beach; large seeds the colors of rust, vermilion, wine, maroon and burgundy, some marked with calligraphy. I collected, one by one, the strays that fell to the ground, hidden in dark corners and cracks. I picked them up learning their names from Ercole; lima bean, butter bean, red kidney bean, Fava, pole, bush and Cannalleni, pinto and Barlotti, Barhunya and Argentin.

And in the tool shed, a different space—a shack, beside the cooling room with padlock to keep me and my brother away from the miscellany of hoes and shovels, pruning hooks, chisels and chains, latches and keys.

We were kept to the threshold, yearning.

Yet nothing of farm life, essentially the production of food, was held from us.

White rabbits for instance, grabbed by the ears and snatched from the hutch, beheaded and skinned, hung from a wire at the tree Dennis and I watched but couldn't describe in drawings or words like *entrails*.

Here we were handed the good luck rabbit foot I didn't ever share with friends back home.

Future warnings murmur in the distance.

The universe of her kitchen with the window sink view of rows of pole beans and potatoes, mounds of beets and kale, and the fish-pond shaped like a figure eight with a tiny bridge we crossed midway to sprinkle fish pellets. Later, tiny minnows appear in vinegar, olive oil, brine—where did she learn this?

Mid-afternoons, customers come to buy our eggs and home-made wine; families living in rentals across the street. Cowboys wearing spurred boots walk up from the rodeo grounds a mile away requesting to buy grandfather's Dago Red. Migrant workers stop for eggs.

But also to envisage the future as visitors paused to embrace the vista and read the text of the land farmed by Italian immigrants equipped with the rural farm skillset to grow more food than they or their family could consume.

Where everyone contributed, workload managed without a *John Deere* tractor, rather relied on hand-hewn work in which the sinew of the arm connects the land, aligned to what it means to have four acres and a shed full of tools.

This life held my grandfather rapt, such that he never lost the joy of the task, a series of processes that enfolded season after season.

I remember our family visited for my grandparent's Golden Wedding anniversary, and to distract me because boys on the schoolyard chased me, and I skinned my knees, grandfather walked me to the cold storage room to show me giant gourds, too heavy to lift, though I tried, harvested for seed to dry and give away.

I remember the arc of blackberries crisscrossing barbwire, my arms dotted with dried blood droplets, the ripe berries out of reach but my brother found a way to crawl under while I pulled back on a vine, sweet and juicy, warmth to melt the scoop of vanilla ice cream.

I remember the delivery of a truckload of sugar beets from Spreckel's Sugar Co. used to fatten a steer, rows of rabbit hutches, neighbors with kids chasing ball on the dust beyond the gravel, an elderly woman in a wheelchair who is found late afternoon at the windowsill surrounded by cats drawn to her consistency like the man who keeps the sugar water bottles full for hummingbirds.

To visit the farm meant you'd eat, fall asleep dreaming, this I realize now.

In this dream customers offer rhubarb or heads of lettuce in exchange vegetables from their gardens, picked by farm workers, vegetables my grandfather won't grow in his own garden to allow the exchange to take place, the gift economy to flourish among his neighbors.

In this way my brother and I learned the dignity of each person living on the borders of Salinas, as were we.

Yet there were other observations including the legend of my maternal grandmother Gene Bonino Airaudi (pronounced Jenny), daughter of Caterina Calvetti, who emigrated to America in 1894 when her husband Giacomo found work in the coal mines of Lehigh, Oklahoma. Choctaw Country is where my grandmother and her two sisters were born though the family returned to Balangero within five years. I never met my great grandmother Caterina, but I adopted her name when I became a writer.

Grandmother Gene, who lived in Redwood City on the Peninsula, told me the story of preparing extra food to share with those who came to California looking for work during the depression. She baked hundreds of loaves of homemade bread to accompany hearty minestrone soup for the hobos who arrived by train at night.

Living off Middlefield in a house my grandfather Domenic built with the help of other Italians, their home was located near the railroad tracks to San Francisco. My mother remembers the tired faces of the itinerant workers who knew they were free to ladle a bowl of soup from the communal pot left out for them on the porch, my mother almost asleep by the time two young men arrived, miles between where they were and where they came from.

Towns, railroad tracks at twilight; niches you left behind, Fortuna, Eureka, and Arcata.

Niches you left behind are a redwing black bird singing from a bulrush in a critical area, culvert in the subdivision turned into marsh where wild things pulse; profuse cottonwood and big leaf maple, blackberry vines looping scotch broom, dandelion, clover, cedar and fir, and swordtail fern because of the rain.

You return as a writer to rescue memory.

Ancestors we did not realize were the bamboo's rustlings roamed among us.

Against the drama of buttes, bobcats oversaw sandstone ledges littered with shale and the miscellany of withered fauna as the morning light gradually formed spheres, and streaks, and other amorphous shapes, mistaken for angels, archangels, and any imagined shape of the remnants left behind, the lost losses of the heart woven loosely within the warp and weft of a frayed text, tattered like burlap, the textile that held things together when the calendar moved to ordinary time, the task to hue memories you come back to as a dreamer, writing.

The poet's hands placed fingertips down on the keys, moving 100 wpm, remembering.

Sometimes you get there by walking, here and now, copy in hand of your current draft, to let the mind riff, confirming cycles of rhythms you've taken for granted; early July for instance, and the deciduous dangle gold earrings of helicopter seeds, evergreens erotically charged, sap running.

Sometimes, it's merely a stage of early childhood, time of autonomy, initiative, industry; a girl, maybe five, six, seven preparing for Holy Communion, mentoring nuns and Father Armstrong, popular priest at St. Pius, altar boys trained to tease while you wait, kneeling for confession, telling the lie that you'll die because you drank the Holy Water in the church vestibule on a dare.

Nun who won't accept what you offer her, the thimble-size vial of the water your father collected from the grotto of St. Bernadette, a refusal you realize is an attempt to undermine your father's credibility, not the legend of the shepherd girl.

I remember staring at my dark brown eyes in the mirror, just a girl, realizing they were beautiful, and if I could just keep knowing this, I would be able to prove how beautiful they always had been, even now.

Sometimes you turn on the computer and what you have is the lit gray screen.

You type as though receiving a message from yourself, tapping it out on the flimsy plastic keyboard, to channel the deeper sediment, click the mouse deleting what is underscored by the psychodynamic underpinnings and vexations; sometimes this both worries and exhilarates, in the groove, not the rut that keeps you stuck.

Sometimes, the nut-brown rabbit in your peripheral vision on the walk, the world there, present, spinning, intoxicated, impinging on your dream like the fallen manzanita branch, silvering the ground.

And, then, again, my brother, Dennis.

Tire spinout, and gravel flecks the muzzle of the stray dog. Not sure where to go. Angular limbs, leathery skin, reddened cheeks, cigar between his teeth. Yesterday the BB gun you use to swat flies, scattering the wrens, wings broken. I was lucky; you aimed the barrel toward the chickadees taking dust baths and not toward my face in the mirror on a hothouse humid August in the valley.

Hallucinations of the hinterlands whose trails prong in multiple directions, embroiled forked forms shrouded by dense fog or burnished haze, rising from the mist a crag revealed, the horizon's scissor cut mountains zigzag the backdrop of reveling, a place never seen before, on the map the trance elevations for quarry and creek, timberline and scat.

And I could not write this landscape without consideration for the Pinnacles, the place I continue to wonder if it exists only in the imagination of my father's stories rife with elk, coyote, white tail deer and the rattlesnake I knew to listen for by the time I was three; Domenic, my maternal grandfather, bitten by a diamond back, rumor he drowned cats in a gunny sack, killed a man in a Butte copper mining camp accused of cheating at liar's poker.

I learned to suck out the venom and tie a tourniquet above the bite.

All I have is the cascade of fragments from my dreaming to help me to make meaning from the lives of the departed men in my family. Men who resided in America a handful of years, savvy of the wilderness, so unlike their homeland.

When I imagine the influence of the environment on my father I must take into account the wilderness of mammals and birds, abundant when he was a boy going to school in Gonzales, Soledad.

By then he would have learned English and continued to speak the Piedmontese dialect and more, it would serve him well to understand others with similar language patterns, migrants from Mexico, neighbors who heard Spanish growing up, and Italians with work visas who would feel welcomed by his friendly disposition, helpful and outgoing manner, here—hot cup of coffee for you, and a map of Yosemite, I'll take you there when you have a three-day weekend—not a problem, you have to see Yosemite.

Lorio the Swiss, his wife Netta and their sons, stopping by the farm on the way back from an unsuccessful trip, rifles loaded in the back of the pickup.

But the Pinnacles, first a national monument and later designated a national park by President Obama, captivated as a place no one could box him in, contain him, a place to stake out his tent, suspend a sack of food from a hook on the trunk of a tree, watchful for what he could watch for.

Sometimes the convergence of wild grass and chaparral conjures my father, all I need is the rustling scent, and the lyrics that emanate from place names, the Pinnacles, as though destined for remembrance. Even now, a dozen years since his passing, I increase my compassion for my father, drawn to his attachment to place, the sacred west propelling him as though he's dreaming again, the dream of another road trip to Yosemite, next summer Yellowstone, when I have three weeks.

California, if not America, I would say, was his place of birth where a boy learned to run, then read. It was here my father loved, made a family with my mother.

Again, the reverie of summer's parched terrain, a water mirage appearing in the distance, yet always out of reach—ahead of us, lulling us forward, promising to quench our thirst, Chevy car windows rolled down as though this lure of illusion will satisfy.

It is the snare of the thing that can't be reached, vanishing the moment I open my eyes, gone the instant I dare believe I can catch the fleeting.

This is the way it is. Something seers into memory—a phrase, tone of voice, fragrance and taste sensory, though more than the well of texture and scent, color and shape.

Remembering brings back feelings to express emotions laden with varying intensities; the original experience meant something, a conveyance, already disappearing as it is remembered, but a presence that is by its very nature a shapeshifter.

This I could not have known as a girl.

I was in the state of becoming, apprentice in the service of the beautiful life, here, not there.

My father knew the sensory liberates.

He learned this as a boy, traipsing the byways between San Miguel and Paso Robles.

His parents a people of gestures.

Their creative work to cook, repair, swaddle; all forms of writing.

And here I'm lost in the reverie, where I no longer understand.

I remember teaching the neighborhood children to play school, organizing makeshift cardboard boxes into desks to face the imaginary under the willow. My friends with their younger siblings in tow told me they wanted to learn to read. Neighbor boy Eddie Velasquez did learn, using both sets of letters, upper and lower, to spell his name and his brother's. Copying words from *Dick and Jane* and the *McGuffey Reader* my grandmother was given to learn to write English.

But on the farm there were no neighbor children; only my brother, eleven months younger, age and gender threading the lattice of childhood.

In this fragment my father is pulled out of the eighth grade to bale alfalfa on the ranch, sweet scent he says he'll never forget when we drive through farm country, scent of alfalfa and timothy on your neck, your clothes; ranch hands smell of cows' milk twice a day between fence mending, catnaps, grub and whistling.

This is the lyric my father sings though there is also silence.

Phases of his life unknown to me between the time he left school and stint in the Navy, maybe fifteen years, two wives, daughter Catherine I never meet.

Bits and pieces when I immerse myself in the art of the era my father lived within, artist age-mates he may have become given the chance.

Photographer Edward Weston with a studio in Carmel, a weathered redwood cabin on the cliffs above Big Sur, renowned photographer of Point Lobos, collage motifs of driftwood hunks tangled in kelp, the Tina Modotti nudes. Modotti, an immigrant the same age as my grandmother, two women who may have crossed the street together in San Francisco where my father was born.

I remember we took Sunday drives; North Beach, Little Italy, across the Golden Gate to Sausalito; pastel pink *Capezio* ballet slippers for sale in shop window, artists on houseboats, clotheslines and easels outdoors. Ansel Adams photos of Yosemite, though I'm not sure if my father knew of either artist, but to know they lived in California, the tenacity to make art.

I was the girl with the big brown eyes shaped like my mother's, but not blue.

Large dark eyes with the topaz flecks I found when I looked closely, through which I observed the world near-sighted until I was given glasses and noticed for the first time the leaves on the maple trees across the street from the optometrist's office were crisply edged, not blurry.

When Dennis and I stood before the mirror in the bedroom we began by making faces, comparing our eyes to one another, color and shape, searching for evidence of the expressive emotional content we were capable of making, close in age, psychically connected, the feminine and masculine version of the other, we might have been twins. There, between the gold flecks of the delicate filigree of the iris, we saw our humanity.

You could say when we made faces in the mirror we paid attention to the similarities and differences to focus us inward, toward ourselves, the nuances that would later become lapses in remembering like the moon waning.

We had not yet betrayed the other, did not yet recognize the shadow, knew only the wonder of the boy, the girl, opposites, yet not, mediated by the land, the language, the family.

The lyric is the desire to breathe underwater, diving for what was forgotten, to rescue this handful of fragments.

To closely observe ourselves, to take careful note of the color of our eyes in the mirror, required that this take place against the backdrop of sun rays lapping through the open window, the bottom pane raised slightly, enamel smell of the freshly painted ecru sill, the pair of billowy wine-colored voile curtains we hid behind to watch our grandmother cut the pink roses for the vase she placed in front of the statue of the Madonna Uncle Frank brought back to her from his annual trip back home to Mexico, bringing this interlude, our performance to a close.

In other words, I didn't know that someday I would understand that the afternoon light, its angle against the window-pane, was essential to the way we saw ourselves.

In a room with no windows we couldn't have enacted this.

In the barn with the feral cats, in the midst of the dark forest, something else would have transpired.

Against the backlight, we were given the mirror of ourselves.

Farm is the landscape of running feet, fog and the barn to gather eggs, my grandmother moving within the borders of the farm, spaces that require different ways of being.

Farm, landscape, scratch, scratch of the hoe, squeak of the wheelbarrow, meeting my grandfather on the path as he's pushing the wheelbarrow and stops to ask me about his family I visited in Montaldo Scarampi.

I laugh, knowing something that he could not know, and I did not know, either; at the time, too young to understand the ramifications of what I knew because I was young and he was no longer young and connected in time and space to that life, having severed something that we didn't know could not be severed, only added to, a dream forged in the living of a life.

Farm, land, irrigation, rain, earth, mud and dust, weeds and vegetables, bamboo a texture to stake and tie, palm fronds we gather to tie and stake, and I'm lost again in the wheel ruts that come up that I need to expand.

Things happen. People reveal themselves. Others ignore or chose to help. Families strive to be accepted, but when pained, withdraw. This is the farm, too, composed of the gambler, the writer, the one becoming an American.

People like Bea and Woody Day; Ray and Ruth Doda; Andrew and Jenny Costa; Frank Vargas, and many others.

To write this lyric is to allow myself the obsession with a plot of land, the town of old cars simmering asphalt, heat waves in the distance.

There was a library built after we left, families forming a path with heavy-tread shoes, the backs of the elders bowed from the work of stooping in the fields, the short hoe my father tried to explain to me was wrong.

When I begin, I'm hooked by the manacles that shaped me like the gopher pulled up in a trap, oblong like a football, its whiskers twitching, my grandfather laughing again, as his shovel, loaded with dirt, filled the hole where he set the trap.

In this memory things run amok, the way it does with time; maybe we're on our way to the 4th of July parade downtown, waiting for Uncle Frank to drive us there, my brother's Godfather. I'm waiting by the car, wearing a spanking new red plaid shirt, disobeying the taboo against playing with the feral cats, cuddling a kitten not knowing she's sick, grandmother unbuttons and slips the blouse off, sombreros, Stetson hats, leather boots, saddles, reins swelling in the streets.

The Salinas Chinese Cemetery on Natividad Road is located next to the eastern border of the farm. Here my brother and I took turns peering out through thickets of bamboo. Sometimes we saw no one, only beginnings of the morning sun struck like a match stick. If we were feeling brave and adventurous we'd leave the confines of the farm and walk out to the road. We held our breath, slipping under the eucalyptus during ceremonies we didn't understand, naughty, where we didn't belong, and weren't supposed to watch the families place their kiln-fired bowls of rice on smooth stones, like nothing we had ever tasted on our tongues, pieces of spicy red peppers and fish oil. I imagine the conversation we might have had deciding whether to remain on our side of the fence. Asking what would happen if the ancestors' offerings were disturbed by two child interlopers, boy eight with buzz cut short and fuzzy, sister nine with long ponytail should-know-better. Believing we would have brought down a heaven of shame, raised Catholic with original sin, beginning to understand venial and mortal sin and this we agreed, clearly of the mortal category. So not to transgress, we hovered, twitching like rabbits in the underbrush, chigger bites up and down our arms and legs, scratches to answer to from brambles grandfather threw in the compost pile between us and their dead who we believed were definitely alive and would upend us if we crossed the invisible line of taboo my grandparents reinforced. What held us together, my family and the people on the other side, was the way the work of farming, the gestures and rhythms of being a farmer, shaped the body, exaggerated it in some places, invigorating for some and breaking others. This my brother and I did not know and couldn't have known then, until years later after we'd both left, not understanding our grandfather who we'd thought would always be there, on the farm, identity intact with a singularity of text and scent exuded, living sculpture of garment, leather, facial features and cigar smoke, taking the walk in the morning as it was his practice to begin early in the day.

Cirrus along the ridge absorbed by low-lying fog, sparrows and crows on the clothesline when grandmother looks out the kitchen window, her hands wet and sudsy from dish washing so perhaps she pulls her sweater sleeve over her hand to help her turn the knob of the back door as she hurries past the memory of when she slipped and fell on the boot scraper. Maybe she wonders why this flashback now, tinge of guilt, Ercole collapsed on the ground in the garden, the wheelbarrow filled with autumn roots, his thoughts vintage wine splashing the future questions: what to grow, when and where to plant, a wife's sweater to cover him before calling their son, my father, Hugo, his hand in hers, marble, tactile, *Andiamo via, I go now, for a while, on a trip.*

It was my fault. I should have known not to climb into the back of the truck. It was what any boy would do, pick up a shotgun and pull the trigger, my younger brother wild, on the edge. Adults forgot children in the garden. My brother's godfather came for us when he heard, me in the backseat beside Aunt Celia. The water given was to bring us back to real time. In the front seat Uncle Frank repeated to my brother you wouldn't want to hurt your sister. I was close range, smiling as though he held a camera. Grandmother walked me to the kitchen for a drink from a glass I watched her fill and drank to show I was alright. We were hidden in the boxwood. Grandfather swore at his friends. When I turned around the farm would never be the same. While the men were inside the house, my brother and I climbed in. I stumbled over sacks of grain, tailgate to the cab window. When I turned away my brother found the rifle. When Dennis called my name, he was pointing the muzzle in my direction and I don't remember his face. In fourth grade I'll meet a boy from Texas out of reform school and baseball players who follow me home for cookies and milk, packs of boys, but not to one do I confide my interpretation of when I was spared.

The water to drink after the gun shot was to draw us back to real time, protected, where accidents don't happen to frighten the elders who couldn't have known.

Accidents happen when adults forget.

Future warnings murmur in the distance.

Something breaks down but we were lucky.

It was a moment when adults forgot children in the garden.

It was my fault.

I should have known not to climb into the back of the truck.

It was what any boy would do, any little brother who'd watched cowboy shows, and my responsibility to realize what he might do.

I've been told the reason the bullet missed me, but I will never understand, only my brother smiling as though holding a camera asking me to smile.

Uncle Frank came for us that evening and we drove back late at night, me in the back seat sitting beside Auntie Celia, her daughter Sandra my age on the other. In the front Uncle Frank kept asking my brother what happened, reminding him he wouldn't want to hurt his sister, saying that over and over as I watched the moon follow us into the night; the burden on my brother to answer for his behavior weighing on me. Until Aunt Celia said *it's late, go ahead, rest against my shoulder*, my mother far away, her daughter soothed by another mother, *dorme, dorme, sleep.*

The farm that summer was stolen but I didn't know it.

In the beginning you string beads as though one idea will easily follow the other in linear order because the primary colors call out to be chosen so that you leave behind the pastels and grays to focus on the bold and resonant that are strong featured, not knowing you'll have to come back to sleuth what was missed, the garden scent, phrase, forgotten incident, meaning.

You already know anything can trigger. Yet you are torn between the desire to go where the prompt takes you and the fear of what it might bring. Writing close to the bone is a form of rock climbing, risky. The terrain draws you in, including spikes in temperature, fire in the distance, smoke moving out to the Pacific. Sometimes the landscape is a place to hunker down as you question, are you using writing to deflect what is unsolvable within the sphere of human relationships?

You think you need to somehow link the passages to allow the readers' coherence. Then you realize you are on the journey you've carved out for yourself. Leaps, synaptic in nature, imagined you here.

In fourth grade I'll meet Casey from Texas, the one to whom I confide my narrative of the accident in which I was spared.

Not to speak shapes the memory.

But this sound is the memory.

When I begin the light is a sheaf of barley the color of goldenrod embroidered wisps along the horizon.

Where there are mountains, dawn's line is broken Morse Code, dashes and hyphenations within the gaps of low elevation luminous things: waterfalls, the Army tent's grommets, those coppery tufts of the cottontail, snakeskin snagged on a sticker bush, abalone shards at the bottom of a beach pail, remnants ablaze, scene of camouflage and wonder.

When I begin the light is a slip of goldenrod, first cousin to black-eyed Susan, Van Gogh sunflowers, intense marigold-orange dye made organically from the bark of alder, carrot roots, and sometimes eucalyptus bark, onion skins and twigs of lilac.

I know this because I played with color dropping fragments of vegetable matter into boiling water then cooling.

The sun a color wheel, reeling between dawn and dusk.

When I begin I don't know we'll never reach the horizon on fire.

I follow the sun like my father.

He drove the car north and dawn stabbed our faces but we did not flinch, blinded on the right so that we were uncertain where we were going, transformed into wanderers though the highway clearly marked.

It was more difficult than we knew for the family of four to take their place in the Volkswagen van.

On my way out the door to kindergarten, my father stopped me from crossing the threshold. Not to give me a hug as I had thought, but to tell me to button my sweater and to listen to the story of when he was a boy and his mother packed his saddlebag with figs and goat cheese, good bread and something he would share with the other children, maybe beef jerky dried on racks in the sun. I looked back promising to ask grandmother. When I did, she gazed out the kitchen window to the land, its barn and corral I never saw, but which she relied on, rooting for her son.

What does it mean to become enthralled by the memories told to you by your father? An invitation, I would say, for someone like me to become the archivist of her father's repository, conduit for a transfer of knowing, the bridge for historical context within its own singularity, the boyhood of Hugo Joseph Bianco and a lesson he learned from the vaquero during the heat of August. For the vaquero is the man my father conjured during the last winter of his life. For what reason I imagine respect, the bond of child to elder, Agostina his mother, willing participant in the fledging of her child.

Maybe some will say I take it too far, romanticizing the ranch, embellished by nostalgia.

On a dark night in December he will recall with rapt intensity as though he is the storyteller at the fire, as though my husband and I were standing out in the afternoon sun with him in the dusty paddock as he was lifted into the saddle and handed a pair of reins.

Maybe they would be right and okay with me; this, a notebook not meant to bring comfort to the reader.

Spring hairbrush memory: Maybe I was nine or ten, during one of the summer vacations on the farm, not wanting my long hair washed and combed out, my grandmother sharing with me the story of her early days in America when she worked for a family with a daughter who had hair a similar color, chestnut brown, reddish, and long waves, my grandmother's job to help ready her for school with tangles combed out braided with pink ribbons, details lost on me as she related the experience of her first job in America, a newly wed, her spouse leaving her behind in New York City to work for a family with a houseful of children while he made his way to California and would call for her. That's all I know, my hair was the same color as that girl, and my grandmother wanted me to know, to imply I too was worth someone who would look after me. There is no more to the story than what I've written, except to say my grandmother had a job where she cared for children in a household that could afford a servant devoted to the task, while she couldn't wait to leave for California to join Ercole and begin their new life. There is no more to this story than what my grandmother said except to say that when she told me about the job of caring for a girl and brushing her hair, I was ten and she was maybe 70, with fifty years gone by since the time of that job and what was not spoken, image of Grandmother at the mirror as she brushes granddaughter's hair, wistful nature of putting words to reflection, the past a wave of associations steeped in longing for the self, for the girl sitting in front of her in the mirror, for a girl, long ago.

In retrospect Yosemite is not a black and white reminiscence but a continuum of the range of dark to light within which there are infinite grays the artist plays like the keys of a piano.

For me, a brown-eyed girl, there was comfort in knowing nothing was lost to the negative.

Why I write this now I don't know except to say pay attention to the bones of a place—why it's interesting, not pretty, photographs by Ansel Adams masterful, each angle a decision toward how to undress the place to essentials, disrobing the scene to make visible the textures of grooves and protrusions on the granite face, for instance. Not to focus on the wildflower, rather reveal snow at tree line against spiral rock; not the nature scene of woodpeckers.

Formidable, massive, and grand, easy synonyms to the page, Yosemite a haunting cataclysm, Half Dome's indelible consciousness of sensory overload that mesmerizes as many are drawn beyond danger signs, cameras in hand, to plunge to their deaths.

We did not beg to go to Disneyland. In the backseat Dennis and I found our sleeping bags. We left before the spires of Pinnacles Monument haloed in light. Against the drama of morning the bobcats oversaw their sandstone ledges littered with fallen rock, the miscellany of withered fauna.

I remember the light formed shapes mistaken for what remained behind. Interior, within the backdrop, muted, like the task to mold, fingers hueing clay.

Light is a workhorse without a proper name, the daily molding of sentences you come back to as a writer.

Where is the map I would turn to so that you could begin to understand the deeper reams of the farm originating in my childhood? Should I begin with another bricolage of recall, or, perhaps, take a different tack, stand with the girl, within the framework of *terroir,* French for the concept that the very soil of a place affects the taste and development of all that grows upon it, especially pertaining to the grapes of a vineyard. How best to describe Salinas *terroir* but record the word *earth, black earth,* tell how low-lying fog and shape-shifter oak become coyote and mustang, my brother standing in a field where the valley is grooved by tractor tines and rimmed by the distant hills that dishevel in waves of erosion, gullies the essence of coastal mountains, my brother leaning against the little hills, to hold them in place, what memory does to you, hold belief in a place. It's dusk. Dennis scoops up handfuls of dirt we toss high up in the air to touch the sun, to glitter the sky.

In my fourth grade classroom my father broke the boundary between home and school, coming into my class to show the films he'd taken of the art he'd seen on my parent's trip to Europe the summer before I entered fourth grade. The room was hot, muggy, afternoon with no air, children restless, hoping for long recess while projector warmed, children drowsy after peanut butter and grape jelly sandwiches.

When my father arrived the curtains were drawn, lights dimmed, taking time mid-day from managing his grocery store to talk to us between the snickers and jests, about the body beautiful, Michelangelo's *David,* in particular, imploring / admonishing us not to laugh, the artist a student of the body like the rest of us, learning his trade 500 years ago, the sculpture of Moses he would strike on the knee to bruise him, form a welt to force him to speak, make marble behave as though human.

This was one of those moments of learning when my father used his authority to teach by showing how he could prove that to travel was the thing no one could take away from you. You could be changed by what you saw, your viewpoint altered and expanded and when that happened you would forever have a responsibility to share of that context. As the black and white film reel ran its course students in my class imbibed sensibilities of the man who would return to Italy in a couple of years with his daughter to make good on the promise of his lesson. I don't know how to explain the father who eventually told my mother to call the pediatrician when, having had a stomach ache for two days, I was diagnosed with appendicitis, the operation scheduled four hours later. I don't know how to reconcile the man who appreciated the body rendered through the artists' work but distanced himself from his eldest born eight years before me, my sister with cerebral palsy from a difficult birth; the juxtaposition of tensions between the image bound within the marble statue and the dynamics which one can't control of the living body that emerge, unfurl, evolve and enfold.

I thought that one day I'd reflect on those experiences that made me a brown-eyed girl crossing the ditch, observer of bordered spaces, narratives.

Last night I returned to the drawer in the basement where I store old maps.

I found the one of Monterey County, the route circular to Arroyo Seco, one of our destinations, because of the morning light that impelled the aesthetic my father was following. His practice to showcase sunrise, capture it, in the hillsides, an outcropping with cougar on the precipice, yes, true. Because I saw it, heading east into morning, an example of *la bella figura*, Italian phrase meaning *to make a beautiful image*, against the foothills, within the shifting elevations that abut the Pacific Coast Range and barricade from the ocean. This would allow us to return by a different route in the evening through Gonzales and Soledad. Boyhood towns of my father he did not avoid, pointing them out to us, a form of cherishing, to breathe in the dust of these dots on the map that whisper his name in the shade of oak weeping acorns to the ground.

We drove the two-lane highway passing through little towns.

Two places merge on the map, though actually not near one another at all when you look closely, and separated by give or take ten miles, the way one town becomes another town, superimposed, the way emotional terrain hovers, trying to engage geographical space, then drifts away, disappearing, then reappears, later in the dream.

Summer Space. Towns. Soledad. Gonzales. Paso Robles. Morgan Hill. Watsonville. Castroville. Monterey. Salinas.

Railroad tracks at twilight; niches you leave behind. The niches you left behind are a redwing black bird singing from a bulrush in a critical area.

The culvert in the subdivision behind the middle school turned into marsh.

Here, wild things pulse the thickets of cottonwood and big leaf maple, blackberry looping scotch broom, dandelion and clover, cedar and fir, swordtail because of the rain.

You return as a writer to rescue memory.

Remembering is what you're doing.

Sometimes you get there by walking, here and now, copy in hand of your latest draft, the mind riffing, affirming the cycles of rhythms; early July for instance, and the deciduous dangle gold earrings of helicopter seeds, evergreens erotically charge, sap running.

Sometimes, it's a stage of early childhood, autonomy, initiative, industry; a girl, maybe five, six, or seven preparing for Holy Communion.

Father Armstrong, the popular priest at St. Pius, altar boys trained to tease while you wait, kneeling for confession, telling the lie that you'll die because you drank Holy Water in the vestibule on a dare.

A nun you adore who won't accept what you offer her, the thimble-size vial of the water your father collected from the grotto of St. Bernadette, a refusal that undermines your father's credibility, not the legend of the shepherd girl.

Salinas, again.

Something in grandfather's question interpreted my response he was one of them, but he wasn't, leaving him of the land, heading down dirt paths to weed vegetables.

The writer puts everything on the line like that day grandfather came toward her with his wheelbarrow and the question, did you see my family?

For now, we're in the dining room waiting for the ice cold bottle of Asti Spumanti to warm slightly to room temp.

We're eager for the cork to pop when the effervescence in the bottle synchronizes with the energy in the room. Tiny, delicate, hand-blown liquor glasses / *bicchierri* set before us.

My brother and I toast with family and friends on the occasion of our grandparents' 50th wedding anniversary.

The back story is my father's warning—*the cork could take your eye out. Don't get too close.*

Something in his question interpreted my response he was one of them, but he wasn't like those people, leaving him heading down a dirt path to weed tomatoes.

Giving me a poetics for why I write how I write the sentence that will carry, that will bridge, that will splice emotion to experience and emotion to memory, the girl, the writer, under sail; she jibes, everything on the line, like that day when grandfather came toward me with his wheelbarrow and the question, did you see my family?

We're in the dining room waiting for the bottle of Asti Spumanti to warm slightly; my father has cut the wire cage that keeps the cork in place.

We are waiting for the cork to pop, delicate glasses set for us at the table and my brother and I toast our grandparents' 50th wedding anniversary.

But my father's warning, the cork could take your eye out, lingers in memory.

Future warnings murmur in the distance.

Don't stop.

This is how fragments are sorted, listless and pale, robust and festooned, so that I won't stop as though all is revealed; some things may never be known.

Make of the pieces what you can.

Part Three

I remember fishing poles and hooks / rainbow trout in the wicker tackle box. Cardboard box of day-old chicks under the stove to keep warm; collecting brown double-yoke eggs. Rattlesnake tail / skin, a talisman saved in poker chip box. Food scraps in a pail; hens pecking order. Raccoons / skunks in the barn. Sun rays on the river rafts. Sunday afternoons at the beach; vanilla wafers and biscotti softened by salt air. Heel of parmesan cheese in kitchen sink drawer to grate for risotto. Radio station set to shows. Italian gazette / Reader's Digest. Collecting palm fronds after a storm. Bull in paddock. Dairy, peacocks, breeding Holstein. Inside the barn to milk and chase cats. Sherwood Forest mushrooms on the way to Monterey. Ordering prune cake from Pink Pastry for birthdays. Gigging frogs in the canal. Mosquito bites that swell my eye shut. Joining hands with Dennis and my cousins to run toward the sunset, horizon aglow. Bea and Woodie and grandfather cleaning up the house after a binge to begin again. Slaughtering the steer. The Graglia's. Tools / sheds / wheelbarrow. Music phonograph and Victrola.

Sewing machine — treadle. What I have is their stories. Valise to America. Poker chips. Wine apparatus. Leaving, driving away. Towels in the hallway closet. One photo of my sister Catherine.

There were stars.

Infinite Blue Nova's; galaxies yet named.

Suns that had died to form us, the pink eyes of the white rabbit bore witness when the summer fog lifted.

When the boy with the sister found the address it was impossible to locate, not the same memory.

Is there one fairy tale that captures?

Because there was the first time when I would have run alone, but my brother beside me trying to keep up, so I held his hand and also my cousins', linking us in the long chain of children who watch the horizon, like birds on a wire.

And, there would have been a time, and someone would have found me, but in the beginning the matchstick ember to focus our gaze as we ran, the azure sky a field through which everything became.

But I do not know if we were right to attend my grandfather's funeral—my daughters didn't know him except for one visit from Florida while I was in college.

What I remember from my childhood is my grandfather thanking me in the dialect of longing for the future I understood wouldn't arrive for
him.

Sometimes, I only remember fence posts on the way to Salinas, boot scraper at the back door, shiny black leather shoes muddied, running
there.

I'm reading Fanny Howe, lost in my own decades, trying to frame a lifespan, offer continuity across historical and sociological interludes that offer a quality of coloratura, subtle nuances of gray charcoal shadings on thick white artist paper. Other times bold outlines wet and shiny like slurry on asphalt, black to accent the trigger was pulled yet no one died, the assassin in shadows in the South where we lived, year my first child was conceived.

Sometimes I have a dream that I'm trapped in a costume with a broken zipper, stuck within the fabric of history interpreted by scholars, pundits, and others who elevate themselves as different, somehow better, because they're of the Greatest Generation.

My father is an Italian. First in his family born in America. Boy who spoke a regional dialect that is today claimed as a distinct language. When he entered first grade at San Gabriel Dam School in 1921, and I have the photo, a black and white of forty students who ranged in age from five to fourteen in a one-room schoolhouse, it was my youngest who noticed the barefoot girls sitting on the bottom step wearing thin cotton dresses, my father in the front row, smiling, the children perhaps asked to say cheese, sing a good morning song that unified the children like the depression, and the war to come.

He is the history of that one-room school house.

For a five-year period, I was always returning home from another road trip to Rose Haven Adult Family Home, a mile from my mother's residence on St. Francis Street where my parents lived since 1950 in Redwood City. During those trips I tried to activate long-term memories, the last to leave us as we age with dementia. I drove with my husband to the Stanford University Mall to walk the aisles of the grocery market with its outdoor bins filled with fresh local organic fruits and vegetables. Plums and lemons reminded me of the farm. I'd bag them up in brown paper along with artichokes from Watsonville, purplish heads of Gilroy garlic, fragrant rustic Italian bread and slender slices of Fontina, his favorite cheese we had once shopped for in our local delicatessen on Woodside Road when I was a girl. Creamy, yet firm, a gourmet imported, and example of terroir so that when we shared during a meal we experienced place. On one of my last visits he and I opened the package of Fontina from the Palo Alto market and broke off a piece from the loaf. We lit a candle. It was dark in his bedroom, December and we would soon be leaving to make it to Portland before Christmas where my daughter and family lived with our two-year old granddaughter. It would take another visit during the summer on the road trip with our youngest daughter for my father to say what had been bottled up for a number of years, *I'm sorry for the trouble with the little one*, a phrase that healed as it astonished, the mystery of words and their power when mustered with eloquence and timing. My father perhaps aware that he must say this to me now, and that it didn't matter about other things anymore.

I remember fence posts on the way to Salinas, a boot scraper at the back door, the black patent leather shoes I muddied, grandfather thanking me, come again, a dialect of longing I understood, nodding. Persistent rain through the Redwoods, floods of ennui the closer we come to Arcata, Humboldt State, Pacific coast towns bound by the past from a promise to myself I detoured away from long ago to live a history of abrupt transitions and leave-taking. I remember my family saying goodbye to Nona Agostina outside the house, my daughters scuffing the toes of their shoes in the gravel and then we drive away toward the ocean to recapture something, like a gull whose wing we had helped to mend. I remember the mirror of the shop and thinking I look way too thin, unaware I'm pregnant. We decide to buy the porch swing woven of hemp; it reminds me of burlap, my grandfather and the farm when I was a girl, gathering eggs and other living things.

www.ingramcontent.com/pod-product-compliance
Lightning Source LLC
Chambersburg PA
CBHW060207050426
42446CB00013B/3017